100 Badass Quotes

Nonia Books

Published in 2024 by Nonia Books
Copyright © 2024 by Avinash Prasad

100 Badass Quotes
ISBN: 978-93-340-6179-6

.

The greatest danger for most
of us lies not in setting our aim
too high and falling short;
but in setting our aim too low,
and achieving our mark.

Michelangelo

It does not matter how slowly you go, as long as you do not stop. Perseverance is key to eventually reaching your goals, no matter the pace.

Confucius

Do not wait to strike till the iron is hot; but make it hot by striking. Take action and create the opportunity instead of waiting for it to come to you.

William Butler Yeats

The greatest glory in living lies not in never falling, but in rising every time we fall. Resilience and recovery from setbacks define true success and strength.

Nelson Mandela

Everyone is where they are at because they worked hard for it. Don't ever hate on someone's hustle. Just figure out how you can get there.

Jo Koy

The best way to predict the future is to invent it. Take control of your destiny by creating your own path and not just waiting for things to happen.

Alan Kay

You don't have to be great to start, but you have to start to be great. Taking the first step is necessary to embark on the journey to greatness.

Zig Ziglar

I attribute my success to this:
I never gave or took any excuse.
Taking responsibility and not
making excuses are crucial for
achieving success.

Florence Nightingale

Your time is limited, don't waste it living someone else's life. Follow your own passions and dreams rather than conforming to others' expectations.

Steve Jobs

Do what you feel in your heart to be right – for you'll be criticized anyway. Following your heart is crucial, despite inevitable criticism from others.

Eleanor Roosevelt

I am not a product of my circumstances. I am a product of my decisions. Your choices, more than your circumstances, shape your life and future.

Stephen R. Covey

Remember that pain has this most excellent quality. If prolonged it cannot be severe, and if severe it cannot be prolonged.

Seneca the Younger

I fear not the man who practiced 10,000 kicks once, but I fear the man who has practiced one kick 10,000 times.

Bruce Lee

He who is unable to live in society, or who has no need because he is sufficient for himself, must be either a beast or a god.

Aristotle

Before you diagnose yourself
with depression or an
inferiority complex, make sure
you're not just surrounded
by assholes.

Sigmund Freud

Success is no accident.
It is hard work, perseverance,
learning, studying, sacrifice and
most of all, love of what you are
doing or learning to do.

Pele

Most of the important things in the world have been accomplished by people who have kept on trying when there seemed to be no hope at all.

Dale Carnegie

Your task is not to seek for love, but merely to seek and find all the barriers within yourself that you have built against it.

Rumi

If you hear a voice within you say 'you cannot paint,' then by all means paint, and that voice will be silenced.

Van Gogh

We cannot solve our problems with the same thinking we used when we created them. Progress requires innovative and transformative thinking beyond conventional wisdom.

Albert Einstein

The ultimate measure of a man
is not where he stands in
moments of comfort
and convenience, but where he
stands at times of challenge
and controversy.

Martin Luther King Jr.

The only place where success comes before work is in the dictionary. Hard work is a prerequisite for achieving success in any field.

Vidal Sassoon

We can't help everyone, but everyone can help someone. Each individual has the power to make a positive impact, no matter how small.

Ronald Reagan

I am not a product of my circumstances. I am a product of my decisions. Your choices, more than your circumstances, shape your life and future.

Stephen R. Covey

Life is 10% what happens to us and 90% how we react to it. Our reactions to events play a far greater role in shaping our lives than the events themselves.

Charles R. Swindoll

Do the difficult things while they are easy and do the great things while they are small. A journey of a thousand miles must begin with a single step.

Lao Tzu

A bird sitting on a tree is never afraid of the branch breaking, because its trust is not on the branch but on its own wings.

Charlie Wardle

The way to get started is to quit talking and begin doing. Action is the foundational key to all success.

Walt Disney

Believe in yourself and all that you are. Know that there is something inside you that is greater than any obstacle.

Christian D. Larson

Life shrinks or expands in proportion to one's courage. Courage is the key to unlocking new opportunities and experiencing personal growth.

Anais Nin

It always seems impossible until it's done. Challenges may appear insurmountable until we tackle them and prove otherwise.

Nelson Mandela

If you have been brutally broken but still have the courage to be gentle to other living beings, then you're a badass with a heart of an angel.

Keanu Reeves

They say you die twice.
One time when you stop
breathing and a second time,
a bit later on, when somebody
says your name for the last time.

Banksy

Opportunities don't happen. You create them. Success is often the result of seizing opportunities rather than waiting for them to come to you.

Chris Grosser

Life is what happens when you're busy making other plans. Embrace spontaneity and live fully in the present moment, for that is where true life resides.

Allen Saunders

Happiness is your nature. It is not wrong to desire it. What is wrong is seeking it outside when it is inside.

Sri Ramana Maharshi

The mind is the root from which all things grow if you can understand the mind, everything else is included.

Bodhidharma

Great is the man who has not lost his childlike heart. Despite life's challenges, maintaining innocence and wonder is a mark of greatness.

Mencius

In the garden of your mind, nurture seeds of compassion, kindness, and wisdom, and watch them blossom into a life of abundance and fulfillment.

Thubten Chodron

In the silence between thoughts, discover the profound wisdom that transcends words and concepts.

Alan Watts

I am not afraid of an army of
lions led by a sheep;
I am afraid of an army of sheep
led by a lion.

Alexander the Great

If you want to lift yourself up, lift up someone else.
Elevate others through acts of kindness and support, for by uplifting those around you, you also uplift yourself.

Booker T. Washington

The purpose of our lives is to be happy. We need to cultivate inner peace and contentment, regardless of external circumstances, to truly experience fulfillment.

Dalai Lama

Through the practice of mindfulness, awaken to the beauty of life unfolding in every breath and every step.

Jon Kabat-Zinn

Do not dwell in the past, do not dream of the future, concentrate the mind on the present moment.

Nagarjuna

Like the bamboo that bends but does not break in the storm, cultivate flexibility and resilience in the face of adversity.

Morihei Ueshiba

All right, they're on our left, they're on our right, they're right in front of us, they're behind us… THEY CAN'T GET AWAY THIS TIME.

Lewis B Puller

The only way to deal with an unfree world is to become so absolutely free that your very existence is an act of rebellion.

Albert Camus

By all means, marry: if you get a good wife, you'll become happy; if you get a bad one, you'll become a philosopher.

Socrates

A little philosophy inclineth man's mind to atheism, but depth in philosophy bringeth men's minds about to religion.

Francis Bacon

If you would be a real seeker after truth, it is necessary that at least once in your life you doubt, as far as possible, all things.

René Descartes

You have to struggle a bit, hustle a little, and be willing to go bankrupt. Once you're willing to do that, everything opens up and you get that freedom.

Nick Nolte

Nothing can stop the man with the right mental attitude from achieving his goal; nothing on earth can help the man with the wrong mental attitude.

Thomas Jefferson

Don't watch the clock; do what it does. Keep going. Persist through challenges by maintaining a steady and continuous effort, much like the relentless movement of time.

Sam Levenson

The best revenge is massive success. Prove your worth not through retaliation, but through achieving outstanding success and demonstrating your capabilities.

Frank Sinatra

When everything seems to be going against you, remember that the airplane takes off against the wind, not with it.

Henry Ford

Never stop being YOU.
I am out to be the best ME
I can be. Do what you LOVE
and you will be badass.

Terry Crews

Successful people have fear, successful people have doubts, and successful people have worries. They just don't let these feelings stop them.

T. Harv Eker

When in doubt, make a fool of yourself. There's a thin line between being brilliantly creative and acting like the biggest idiot on earth.

Cynthia Heimel

Do the difficult things while they are easy and do the great things while they are small. A journey of a thousand miles must begin with a single step.

Lao Tzu

Having the positive belief that it will all be OK just means that you hustle and make it work because failure isn't even an option in your own mind.

Natalie Massenet

You have enemies? Good.
That means you've stood
up for something,
sometime in your life.

Winston S. Churchill

He is a man of courage who does not run away but remains at his post to fight against the enemy.

Socrates

Hardships often prepare ordinary people for an extraordinary destiny. Overcoming difficulties can lead to remarkable outcomes and personal growth.

C.S. Lewis

The greatest weapon against stress is our ability to choose one thought over another. Changing your mindset can be the most effective way to combat stress.

William James

There is no such thing as absolute certainty, but there is assurance sufficient for the purposes of human life.

John Stuart Mill

I'm tough, I'm ambitious,
and I know exactly
what I want. If that makes me
a bitch, okay.

Madonna

It is our choices that show what
we truly are, far more
than our abilities.
The decisions we make reflect
our character more accurately
than our inherent talents.

J.K. Rowling

Pain is temporary. It may last a minute, or an hour, or a day, or a year, but eventually it will subside and something else will take its place. If I quit, however, it lasts forever.

Lance Armstrong

Never be afraid to fall apart
because it is an opportunity
to rebuild yourself the
way you wish
you had been all along.

Rae Smith

All growth depends upon activity. There is no development physically or intellectually without effort, and effort means work.

Calvin Coolidge

No matter how many mistakes you make or how slow you progress, you are still way ahead of everyone who isn't trying.

Tony Robbins

All entrepreneurship really is,
is coming up with an idea,
and then having a lot of hustle
and just doing it.

Amy Nelson

You've gotta dance like there's nobody watching, Love like you'll never be hurt, Sing like there's nobody listening. And live like it's heaven on earth.

William W. Purkey

Don't worry about whether things will be hard. Because they will be. Instead, focus on the fact that these things will help you.

Ryan Holiday

Life is not measured by the number of breaths we take, but by the moments that take our breath away. Cherish extraordinary experiences over mere time spent.

Maya Angelou

You have power over your mind — not outside events. Realize this, and you will find strength. Focusing on what you can control empowers you to overcome external challenges.

Marcus Aurelius

When something bad happens,
you have three choices.
You can either let it define you,
let it destroy you or let it
strengthen you.

Kay-Marie Fletcher

Be the change that you wish to see in the world. Instead of waiting for others to make a difference, take matters into your own hands and lead by example.

Mahatma Gandhi

I am not afraid of storms, for I am learning how to sail my ship. Adversity is a learning opportunity that strengthens our abilities and prepares us for future challenges.

Louisa May Alcott

One of the lessons that I grew up with was to always stay true to yourself and never let what somebody else says distract you from your goals.

Michelle Obama

The only thing we have to fear is fear itself. Facing our fears head-on rather than allowing them to control us is crucial for overcoming obstacles and achieving our goals.

Franklin D. Roosevelt

Rule #1: F*ck what others think. Bite more than you can chew, You're grinding hard; you don't have time to worry about others opinions on your choices.

Avinash Prasad

If you would not be forgotten as soon as you are dead and rotten, either write things worth reading or do things worth writing.

Benjamin Franklin

The question isn't who is going to let me; it's who is going to stop me. True determination means not waiting for permission, but confidently pursuing your goals regardless of obstacles.

Ayn Rand

Success is not final, failure is not fatal: it is the courage to continue that counts. Perseverance in the face of obstacles defines true success, more than any single achievement.

Winston Churchill

Can you imagine yourself in 10 years if instead of avoiding the things you know you should do, you actually did them every single day – that's powerful.

Jordan Peterson

One can choose to go back toward safety or forward toward growth. Growth must be chosen again and again; fear must be overcome again and again.

Abraham Maslow

Everyone who's ever taken a shower has had an idea. It's the person who gets out of the shower, dries off and does something about it who makes a difference.

Nolan Bushnell

Don't mistake my kindness for weakness. I am kind to everyone, but when someone is unkind to me, weak is not what you are going to remember about me.

Al Capone

There are two types of people who will tell you that you cannot make a difference in this world: those who are afraid to try and those who are afraid you will succeed.

Ray Goforth

I will breathe. I will think of solutions. I will not let my worry control me. I will not let my stress level break me. I will simply breathe and it will be okay because I don't quit.

Shayne Mcclendon

Your health account, your bank account, they're the same thing. The more you put in, the more you can take out. Exercise is king and nutrition is queen. Together you have a kingdom.

Jack LaLanne

Success in business requires training and discipline and hard work. But if you're not frightened by these things, the opportunities are just as great today as they ever were.

David Rockefeller

Don't worry, be crappy. 'Revolutionary' means you ship and then test... Lots of things made the first Mac in 1984 a piece of crap – but it was a revolutionary piece of crap.

Guy Kawasaki

Life isn't about waiting for the storm to pass, it's about learning to dance in the rain. It's about finding joy and beauty even in the midst of adversity, and embracing every moment with courage and grace.

Vivian Greene

Life is a battlefield, and I'm a warrior born to conquer. I thrive in adversity, turning every challenge into an opportunity to showcase my strength, resilience, and unyielding spirit.

Serena Williams

Be daring, be different, be impractical, be anything that will assert integrity of purpose and imaginative vision against the play-it-safers, the creatures of the commonplace, the slaves to the ordinary.

Cecil Beaton

Do not let what you cannot do interfere with what you can do. Focus on your strengths and abilities, harnessing them to overcome challenges and achieve your goals despite any limitations you may face.

John Wooden

Twenty years from now you will be more disappointed by the things you didn't do than by the ones you did do. So throw off the bowlines, sail away from safe harbor, catch the trade winds in your sails.
Explore, Dream, Discover.

Mark Twain

9 789334 061796